A DIARY OF LIFE

Edited by

Heather Killingray

First published in Great Britain in 1998 by
POETRY NOW
1-2 Wainman Road, Woodston,
Peterborough, PE2 7BU
Telephone (01733) 230746
Fax (01733) 230751

HB ISBN 1 86188 686 1
SB ISBN 1 86188 681 0

FOREWORD

Although we are a nation of poetry writers we are accused of not reading poetry and not buying poetry books: after many years of listening to the incessant gripes of poetry publishers, I can only assume that the books they publish, in general, are books that most people do not want to read.

Poetry should not be obscure, introverted, and as cryptic as a crossword puzzle: it is the poet's duty to reach out and embrace the world.

The world owes the poet nothing and we should not be expected to dig and delve into a rambling discourse searching for some inner meaning.

The reason we write poetry (and almost all of us do) is because we want to communicate: an ideal; an idea; or a specific feeling.

Poetry is as essential in communication, as a letter; a radio; a telephone, and the main criteria for selecting the poems in this anthology is very simple: they communicate.

'The Diary Of Life' cries out to the reader and gives them a glimpse of the turmoil and wonders of life which the poets have managed to create in this collection of poems. We are able to glimpse into their minds and see their perception of life.

The collection comes together well, into a book which will inspire the dedicated poetry lover or the first time reader. The poems are written on a variation of topics from joyous emotions to everyday grief.

Take the collection, relax and let yourself be inspired by the excellent works that have been brought together in this short but beautiful 'Diary Of Life'.

CONTENTS

FIFTY SCORE

The millennium is in our midst,
The wonders of one thousand years,
Secrets of man's life upon this earth,
Overwhelming hopes and fears.

The lies the truths, loves and hates,
Of man long since gone,
Supply the very essence we build our life upon.

Rulers, monarchs, men seeking power, have been the way of life,
Fighting for boundaries and religion, with years of bitter strife.

But, through all one thousand years,
They saw the same old sun,
They gazed up at the same old stars.

Were the battles really won?

Life was not meant for one man, with all his claims and rules.
To blindly follow tyrants, can only be for fools.

Our seeds are sown to take life, through another fifty score
And hopefully go on and on
And on, forever more.

Ken Lowe

NINETEEN NINETY EIGHT

Some years ago, advisers said,
    'Beware, prepare for Culture Shock!'
We watched the screen, TV was seen
    With spaceships on their way to Mars,
By stars and galaxies.

But Uncle George, in days of yore,
    He laboured on, with horse and drays
On dairy farm, in peaceful days.
    He'd watch the moon and know the weather
From the winds upon the heather
    And on lunar landing, cried
'Oh no! These pictures falsified.
    The moon is much too far away,
Impossible!' he sighed.

Yet he was born in ninety three,
    During previous century,
Which isn't very long ago.
    I wonder just how much we'll know
And what will our reaction be
    To morrow's new technology?

Winifred Mary Richardson

TOO LATE

He took her back to the Shetlands
Where the air is fresh and clean,
Where the biting wind can cleanse one's soul,
Where the sea birds whirl and keen.

She went with him to the islands,
To Fetlar, Unst and Yell,
Away from commuters' frantic strife
And the city's noisome smell.

Where the skylark sings with abandon
And the quartz glints on the shore,
Where the inky sea can drown one's grief
And still come back for more.

But she grieved away from the city,
She missed the traffic's roar,
She yearned for another's hand in hers.
Her nerves were stretched and raw.

She left him alone to the wildness,
To the hill sheep and the burn.
He watched her go with aching heart.
He knew she'd not return.

She sometimes thinks of the islands
And the man who took her there,
When the crowded tube trains rattle and stink
And she's faint from lack of air.

But it's too late now, as the song goes,
Too late to have regrets.
She married into city life.
No time for dreams or frets.

Ann Mather

BACK TO THE EARTH

I open the door; a light breeze lifts my hair;
I pause and reflect for a while,
As my senses take in the sweet rain-scented air
I recall years ago, and I smile.

Once a year, in the autumn, on nights such as this,
I'd make my way through rustling leaves
Down my dark garden path, like the blackest abyss,
To build twigs and dried grass into sheaves.

With a crack and a splutter the match lights my palm,
But the flame gutters out in the breeze.
'Try again girl,' I mutter, trying to be calm,
Then a new flame is born with more ease.

Oh remember the way the flame curls the dry grass;
Remember the wood-scented steam,
Remember the hiss of the rain and the gas
As the green branches heat through and scream!

Well, the law says I can't have such fun anymore,
Here in the year of two thousand and three,
And I understand too - really . . . it's just a bore!
Yet the fire in my heart still burns free!

I pile on some prunings and hear the flames roar;
Find old Michaelmas daisy tops near;
They can't stop me this time - at a quarter past four
In the morning - I'll pay later I fear . . .

I'll just lie on the earth, for a minute's release,
While the air gathers dew by the pyre.
I would like, if you please, to be left here in peace,
It's so lovely and warm by the fire . . .

Jay

NEVER THAT SECOND CHILDHOOD

The moon as it wanes
is a slither of silver,
gathering flowers
to lay beside you.

Laughter.
Some men never reach their prime.
Never that second childhood.
They are gathered up too quickly,
taking sweetness with them.
They hoot and laugh
at the meaning of death
as though it were some fable
written for other men.
But that is the story
they take with them,
when life is cut off too soon.
Their every gesture is remembered
as vividly as today.
So swiftly they are taken
that you can still hear their laughter,
as they seem only to have
walked into the other room.

Linda Anne Landers

A DIARY OF LIFE

Life is as an empty book each phase an unwritten page
We write our story as we go along from age to age

Monday is the baby so helpless and so small
Gazing out upon the world from his cosy shawl
Totally dependant for his daily care
Rewarding with his trusting smile to show he's glad you're there.

Tuesday he's the little boy with rosy face so bright
Going off to school each day to learn to read and write
Playing games and having fun his days pass happily
He gives no thought to what may come, he's just content to be.

Wednesday he's the adolescent, taken quite a stride
Heading for the adult world mature and dignified
Being neither child nor grown up in these teenage years
The future looks exciting but he must have certain fears.

Thursday he's the married man with family of his own
Giving them the love and care which once to him was shown
Watching them as they in turn grow up and spread their wings
And venture out into the world to see what fortune brings.

Friday he's much older now, a grandchild at his knee
So much like his eldest son when he was only three
He lives life at a slower pace but still with certain pleasure
His shoulders bear less burden so he has more time for leisure.

Saturday he's grown very old and spends more time alone
He sits and reminisces of the days that now are gone
He has so many memories of his journey through the years
The failures and successes, the laughter and the tears.

Sunday is the epilogue and he must be assessed
His story is completed, how has he stood the test
What will he be remembered for, what memories remain?
If only for the love he brought he has not lived in vain.

Betty Curnow

MY LIFE ON TRACK

Beginning in the noisy terminus of war
Amid the dust and smoke of other's lives
My little train set out to make its trip
At the Controller's call.

Soon running from the town to country fields
It picked up speed; and then the gradients came
With 'O' and 'A' levels, and then degrees
To test its motive power.

Its journey marked with junctions and with points
Proceeded now in cutting, now on bridge
And reached a cross-shaped gantry, took the line
Where green light answered 'Yes'.

Emerging from love's tunnel once again
The railway now on level paths would run.
And better too. For, looking at the rails,
They now were double-tracked.

And later on, at stations on the way
Branch lines would tend their curving route away
Making for destinations I would pass
Where I could never go.

Downhill towards the sea the train now runs
Past rocks and crags - achievements I have won.
It still has many miles before it comes
To blow out final steam.

And as it nears the final terminus
And to the sidings the old train is pulled
A junction to a new bright line appears
The way into Christ's heaven.

Mike Smith

PRUNING

So Mrs Cuthbert's gone?

Last time I saw her, in the grocer's shop,
She was exchanging views with management,
'Where would you be without me chasing you?'
And then that stare, as straight as anything.
Her next, and last to me,
'Your garden's grown so tall, I had a look.
Don't you go out this weather catching cold:
It gets you in the toes. Well, off with you -
Remember me to Mother. How is she?'

Today I can return that sound advice
As classic mourners gather on the green,
'Don't you go out this weather catching cold.'
And I am up a ladder pruning trees,
The shoots I cut all straight and youthful still.
Last time she walked that grass she used a stick
And laboured somewhat but she made her ground.

I did not know it was her turn today.
The legs that carry her towards the church
Are strong and purposeful, as when a girl
She strode uphill towards a better world.

You'd better get that garden done, she says.

Alasdair Aston

SUNDAY AFTERNOON

Visitors arrive with unnatural brightness.

Through the door a layered smell
chokes nostrils fresh from open air,
permeates clothes, rooms and halls.

Like some cruel obstacle race
walking frames lie scattered
waiting to be used
for bed, or toilet visits.

Grey faces, hair to match,
turn to look, expectantly.
Some, by habit, watch
an unresponsive screen
but some eyes still shine with hope
not yet dimmed by boredom; drugs.

Rowdy, reluctant children
invoke excuses for
hasty farewells.
Is it that time?

Until next weekend then . . .

Grey faces with hair to match
turn in upon themselves again.

Carron Ogden

THE EXILE

Rain-laden clouds
Billowing through the sky.
Wailing, screaming gulls
Blown and dashed ahigh.
Spray splashed, salt cracked
Desolation and a sigh.

Mist shrouded hills.
A watery winter's day.
Bleak, isolation
Weeping, grizzled, grey.
Sea-slapping, spume spraying
Homeland drifts away.

Grasping last moments
Storing images to keep.
Shoreline disappears,
Spirit starts to weep.
Seaward sailing, sanctuary seeking,
Condemned to sleepless sleep.

Released from deep within the soul
A gaping, anguished cry
Is caught upon the surging wind
Thrust to the squally sky.
Surf skelped, scream spliced.
Diffused. Diminish. Die.

Tessa Challenger

YESTERDAY'S DAWN

Our footsteps sound loudly
on streets not paved with gold.
Aspirations lie scattered,
only cinders tell of earlier flames.
Memories are crushed cigarette-ends
as we filter forgotten events
through fictional falsity,
seeking the comforting arms
of fantasy.
But all that we touch crumbles to dust,
like some perverse Midas.
From far off, the streets shine
in the smooth sheen of slow rain;
a surface reflection.
Distantly it hums,
its alluring notes draw us
like sailors into shifting seas.
We cannot cover our ears
and we go willingly,
returning to streets
never as golden as yesterday's dawn.

Christopher G Vowles

ADVENTURER

Small child, adventure burning in its eyes,
It is an explorer of the urban jungle,
With the concrete swamps, electric trees, the street corner savages
And the man-eating, tail swishing tabby cats.

Proud domains, castle upon castle,
Terraced palaces in the grassy gardens,
Lions on guard, straining at the leash.
And journeys in the garages with a broom for a lance
And a prancing wild bicycle beneath you.

Small child, stepping over the cracks in the slabs,
Fearing the fires of hell between the gaps.
Old man is the devil, old woman a witch.
The daily perils of going to school,
The monster cars and the danger of assassins
Dwindle when Mother comes too.

The tarmac playground as a storm-tossed sea,
Where your galleon sets sail for a faraway land.
With sharks to port and a sea monster with goggles -
Mr Bond, the maths teacher - threatening ahead.
Fate has truly been unkind this day,
Plot a different course and sail away.

Saraid O'Neill

ALL THE WORLD'S A STAGE - THE 8TH AGE

And yet, upon the surrender of his cumbersome physical form,
The taking of the last bows; the last scene, sans everything,
Gives rise to the everlasting memory, an existence
To endure the infinite age of time.
On one hand this serves to ignite a blazing fire,
Which illuminates the horizon of glorious immortality;
Yet the moral sense of his perpetual trespasses
Spawns the spectre of an alternative, inanimate world.
This world bears not the name of prosperity, but spans
The painful eternity of each hour
With the imperishable presence of vicious demons,
To inflict constant torture upon his Godforsaken soul.

Sarah J Scott

THAT CERTAIN AGE

'Congratulations,' now you're forty,
So come on, join the club,
Don't mooch around all miserable,
Find solace in the pub,
For life begins at forty,
At least, that's what folks say,
And man, is in his prime of life,
Gets wiser day by day,
The little things, that used to cause,
You upset, or despair,
You'll now, sort out quite easily,
And never turn a hair,
A quick look in the mirror,
Won't make you, grin with pride,
Although, you have some time to go,
Before, the great landslide,
Too soon you'll see, a shiny head,
And then the waistline, starts to spread,
Your chest is where your stomach should be,
It's called, the 'force of gravity',
Till then, enjoy your birthday fuss,
Don't let it be a bane,
For when you're fifty, or sixty plus,
You'll wish you were forty, again . . .

June Fricker

SEVEN DECADES

Behind, the guns had roared their hate; now fretting coal was dust
between the miners' bottled tea and starving kids. A hero's world.

The twenties years. Laughed-at-tweenies, gelded by
the dole house boss, whose frantic
nympho daughter, nimble fingered
to satisfy an ache for other loins.

A peal of guns again.
Gaunt-faced men chewed polished rice
and starved; and Jewry cough-gasped
Cyclon B. Multi-coloured fought
across the multi sweated earth.

Then built an all enveloped wall.
Cold the ice of ice cold war;
super-heated hydrogen hid deep
to rocket earth to paradise.
Korea, Nam and Bethlehem,
helped raise the dead again.
Gulags flourished, crushing thoughts
of tainted men; when suddenly,
coitus; the super states climaxed.

Today, universality. One state, one mind.
Language bates and Euro coins debate
the future. Frontiers open and flood the world.
And coke and grass become the ecstasy of life.

These decades have slipped so fast
and little left to sigh the years away.
Sans Nuit St George,
sans femme,
sans canticle.
What wasted thoughts to justify a lifetime's waste.

L A McIntosh

LIFE

Thrown into the world without choice,
No knowledge of what we will face,
Through tumbles and pain we grow stronger,
And strive not to be a disgrace,

We gain knowledge from our efforts,
Through perseverance we're still easily broken,
Yet we claim the right to love,
Our commitment is then spoken.

We, in turn, create new life
And work ourselves into ease,
Deliberating between our time and comfort,
And remembering the need to please.

But soon our rival faces us,
Age forces us to be slow,
Our function is now less important
Just wait, for what, we don't know.

We face new pain and strife now,
And fear for what we will meet,
But our child-like yearning incites in us,
A desire and need to retreat.

Emma Ormond

HARD TO FIND

Old age: a citizen of senior rank: advanced in years:
Whichever is politically correct
Means limbs always in dilatory mood - sometimes in pain.
Where have I left that stick behind this time.

Mind fully stretched to keep all things intact.
Resorting more and more to memories of the past.
New bright ideas seem hard to grasp - I wonder why.
Sight is a mist with spectacles mislaid
Hearing a perpetual diminuendo - must get an aid.

Determination freely spiced with common sense
Helps keep this dreaded state of age at bay
But please where do they keep a store
Of that illusive thing I need so much called patience.

Phyllis Moore

LEST WE FORGET

So tired and so weary, she worked till the end,
Caring for others, the poor people's friend.
She tended the sick, the hungry, the lame,
Mother Teresa that was her name.
For her courage and valour, it was no surprise,
When she was awarded the Nobel Peace Prize.
Mourned by millions, both young and old,
The Saint of Calcutta, with a heart of gold.
A dear old lady, who was second to none,
Who'll be so sadly missed, now she's passed on.
Mother Teresa, who gave so much love,
Laid finally to rest, in heaven above.

Mary Louise Ainscough

TIME PASSING

January, life is born
To laugh to cry to stretch and yawn.
February, the sight is clear,
An understanding does appear.
March, the feel of touch is strong
With love and life and lullaby song.
April next, a sunny springtime
Filled with flowers and warm red wine.
May has talents with gifts to view
Bringing love that's still brand new.
June is filled with roses fine
July and August, summertime.
Sad September soon comes along
And life's debts are nearly due.
October time is colder
And strain shows in the eyes
That look now on November skies.
All too soon arrives December
But with loving thoughts we will remember
That time will come then pass away
Leading to that glorious day
When loved ones who have passed before
Stand waiting at that open door
Saying, come on in, we know the way
To another brighter January day.

Constance I Roper

ALONE

I am living
But it is no life
I am giving
But not as the wife
I still long to be

It is possible to fill each long day
It's even possible to sleep the night away
But how do you keep from falling apart
How do you ease the terrible pain of being
Without you

Nothing can replace
The pleasure of your hand upon my shoulder
The joy of your step in the hall
The comfort of your hand in mine
The brightness of your smile
The happiness of sharing time
With you

A widow is an empty shell
She walks, she talks, she smiles
And even laughs
But most of all she cries
And feels cheated
Cheated of the dream of growing old
Together.

Barbara Wallace

GROWING DOWN

I recall when I became a man
I laid to rest my Peter Pan
And banished him to my awfully adult child exclusion zone
I thought it was hip to be mature
Melancholic and act demure
But reality shows that I'd simply become a clone
Now this rhyme has too many words
And the metre and scan are absurd
But it's honest about failure and my pain
I'm growing down instead of up
Joy overflows in my cup
Thank God I'm becoming a child again
Computers dominate my house
But in a cage I put the mouse
Named him Harold fed him little munchy things
And I painted a *piktur* pretending to be eight
It was yuck but I thought it was great
And I played in the park on the roundabout and swings
So I'll dress up, don't dress me down
From the dressing up box I'll become a clown
And be like baby Jesus - honest meek and mild
Suffer little children to come unto me
The little children at least are all free
And my adult will be innocent like a child
I recall when I became a man
Said RIP to Peter Pan
And buried childish memories in my next door neighbour's lane
But a key has opened up the lock
And I'm looking in the toy box
And I'm sewing back that shadow once again.

F McFaul

CYCLE OF LIFE

Each death is a birth . . . each birth a death:
As each plant's energy quietly and imperceptibly ebbs in
the fall, and rises in the spring, behind the facade reflecting
the season of its time, without force or show, comes growth.
Each of its changing images signifying a death, each metamorphosis
a birth. Likewise man wears nature's mask of revolving cycles,
Abandoning many cloaks before his welt slowly edges clear.

I stood boundless within the beauty of the vale of light,
where grains of time fall into phials charged timeless
within the weal of life's rotund. Yet, observing the harlequinade
below, I ached to rebirth, relearn grow - shake free the
discontent from within my content. The price; my soul,
or rather its facet I most recent knew. It was time to move on.

I awoke . . . safe . . . secure, Adam with his eve - an entophyte
lodged with a brine - sugar cell, sensing life through a vicarious
impasse, Yet receptive beyond my host's wildest imaginings,
Dancing along the teasing edge of a chariot blade, My entombed
learnings stored within the womb of my rebirth, Ready for my next
entrance, Ready for my emergence into the sphere of dark light;

An innocent tabula rasa held by the soiled hatch - bandages of
a nether life, Programmed to be loved, coddled and pampered,
in a world of false security, Then released into the naked womb
of folly - adolescent rodomontade despair.

Then onward into adulthood, Obstacles, challenges and pain
endlessly tearing at the core of my being, Waltzing with life,
yet never quite following in synchronised step, Missing opportunities
within the quick of every score, Sometimes regretting my passage into
tormented dreams, But always striving to hold onto the roots of
my being, Roots secured with the essence of the promise of
eternity's tomorrow.

Ivan Sanders

MORTALITY

I have had
Such a lesson
In mortality
That it has left me
Totally confused.

I thought that I had,
In a small way,
Come to terms
With my ageing process.
The gradual stiffening of limbs
And loss of memory.

My friend, my travel mentor,
Thinker through,
Keeper of unusual opinions
And facts,
Has aged more than
I wish to know.

It is saddening
To see such decline
In someone I have
Admired and loved
So much,
Particularly as I know
I will be following
The same path.

Chris Malcomson

Rest In Peace

Let us open up our hearts
For our mortal souls soon part
Time so short 'til we depart
Living has become an art

Soon our time here will be done
Though it seems we've just begun
Fond remembrance few or none
Now the judgement day has come

Time to depart this fatal earth
The time has gone for what it's worth
Death upon us from our birth
Now to face an unknown turf

In prison here on earth I've been
Although I've been quite free of sin
A battle I could never win
I suffered solely for my kin

A peacefulness upon me lies
For now I'm closing both my eyes
To face the future that belies
Away from earth I'll surely rise

Zita Holbourne

THE THREE VISITS

Confusion
Last day I walked a rocky shore,
But add to my wisdom, it did no more.
Along this shore I walked,
Walked, even talked
Through my mind,
But e'er did I find
What I was looking for.

Contentment
This day I visit a green, green hill,
My heart with pleasure, it did fill.
This hill I paced,
Paced, my thoughts raced
Across thy head,
And none that's said
Can cause any ill.

Hope
Next day I'll climb the mountain peak
To find the happiness that I seek.
Up the mountain I shall rise,
Rise, through those lies
That haunt thy memory,
And then you shall see
I am no longer the meek.

Christopher Guinness

To Our Senility

When the jaded days have massed and merged
Into years when loves turn likes;
When ageing steps are singly urged,
Before the long dark strikes;
When our shrunken bodies shrink away
From pleasures then dubbed sour,
And our crabbed minds hark to yesterday:
Remember this one hour.

When the slow blood courses sluggishly,
And the cold hands clutch for heat;
When the shuffling steps turn childishly
To the nearest sunny seat:
Gaze on the unchanging sun above,
And think, from your old decline,
How the white fire of your young love
Burnt with the red of mine.

Joyce Barton

ALL IN A DAY

Molly is dead
Yesterday she planned the future
With boundless energy
Blazing stamina
Laughing.

Molly is dead
Laid out in a coffin
Slowly decaying
Force spent
Extinguished.

Molly is dead
Her book of life closed with a slam
Irrevocable
Absolute
Final.

Partner crumples
Caves in
Daughter shocked
Into silence
Death came as a thief
An opportunist
Stamped out her life
Just for the hell of it.

Mair H Thomas

PERHAPS THEY'LL MISS ME

I am so old, I am so sad,
I am so lonely, since I lost *Dad*.
I loved him so, but I must go on,
I miss him now that he has gone.

We'd been together for many years,
And lived through war, heartbreak and tears.
Life is empty without my man,
I want to join him, if I can.

The house is cold, with not much food,
Sounds depressing, so is my mood,
The *kids* don't visit, now they're wed,
Perhaps they'll miss me, when I'm dead.

They just don't care about their mum,
As I sit and wait, for death to come.
I look about the empty room,
And hope *the end* will be here soon.

Lynn Bond

ON GETTING OLDER

Slowly, slowly tick the hours
Inexorably away.
Life which seemed so long when young
Gets shorter by the day.

What have I achieved in it?
Is there anything to show?
Wealth and status I have none,
Nor prizes in a row.

Quickly, quickly try to do
The things one's left undone.
Sample all untried pursuits
Before the end has come.

Slowly, slowly realise
The bond that one has forged
With family and with one's friends
Is its own reward.

Patricia Eales

LOST YOUTH

Like echoes of a distant radio
Which ebbed and flowed on summer evening air,
The strains of record music from a fair
Stirred memories of forty years ago.
Then, round the dodgems we would circle, slow;
Our hub, where fifties rock-and-roll would blare.
Just callow, acned lads with Brylcreemed hair,
Who fancied that some special girl might show.

Beguiled by tempting promises and smiles
On fate's uncertain ride, we ventured far
Down roads forewarned we never should have gone.
What choice between a few rough, chancy miles
And sitting, waiting in life's dodgem car
For someone else to turn the current on!

Terry Edwards

SEPTEMBER BLUES

I've got those old September . . .
Only remember . . .
Through to December blues.

Work, work, work. Shouldn't be a chore
But here and now it's just a bore,
And then the buggers give me more.

I've got those grey September . . .
Dark as November . . .
Through to December blues.

These are the days I always lose;
Get it wrong whatever I choose;
The answers never lie in booze.

I've got those old September . . .
Never surrender . . .
Through to December blues.

But now it's only May!

Robin Brumby

REMINISCENCE

I look down the years
Through the smiles and the tears
And I long for my youth again,
When skies were blue or skies were grey
We activated each new day.

When crystal sets were new born toys,
With television far away,
Few cars and fewer aeroplanes,
Just wagonettes and charabancs,
And tramcars clanging on their way;
The barrel organs on their beats,
The hawkers calling down the streets,
The cowboys on the silent screen.

With crude equipment we pursued
Our outdoor sport with guileless play,
It mattered little which side won,
Just taking part was half the fun.

Indoors with kitchen gadgets rare
The daily drudgery began,
With slaving over blistering stoves,
And washing piling up in droves.

And in the evening gloom we played
Our family games with harmony,
Blow football, dominoes and nap,
And snakes and ladders, draughts and snap.
Then supper time, and time for dreams.

Dreams. Dreams.
Though hope stayed high,
Reality was all around,
With dole queues lengthening to the ground.

I look down the years
Through the smiles and the tears
And I wonder . . .

W H Hodkinson

TRUE LOVE

I met a girl
I fell in love
I thought it was requited
She kissed me once
We kissed again
But then my love was blighted . . .

I sent a card
It was returned
I sent a note
It was rejected.
I sent a rose
My love it burned.
I really had expected
My love would melt
And take me back.
Her back she turned
She walked away.

She flees from me
As from a plague
A virulent infection.
But all I did
Was fall in love
Though, childlike would not see
That love is not true love
That binds
The one who would be free.

Joyce Goldie

THE BALLAD OF THE FIELDS

In feudal times, it was three strips -
Wheat, barley, oats or rye,
One strip left fallow in every field -
That was good husbandry.

Some fields were full of woolly sheep,
For wool was England's trade,
And the Chancellor sat on the great Woolsack
When the laws of England were made.

The May Queen was crowned while the children danced
On the patch of the village green,
While on holidays there were jousts and tilts
Where knights in armour were seen.

The country was Merrie England then,
And farmers still lived on their lands;
They tilled their fields and grazed their stock
And lived by the work of their hands.

Then machinery took over the farms,
So men sought work in the town,
When fields were enclosed by the squire's decree,
Or were forfeit to the Crown.

We loaned the fields in the years of war
To the men who fought in the air,
But lesser fields were ploughed and sown
And provided our war-time fare.

And now there are rambling clubs and reserves
Where flora and fauna hold sway,
And football has swallowed up vast tracts of land,
With other ball games that men play.

But whatever the usage from age to age
Our fields will remain our heritage.

Teresa Finlayson

GOLD AGE

Most people, like good wine
Will improve with age
When, in the book of life
They reach the final page

Not spoiled and embittered
By the ravages of time
But full-bodied, rich and sweet
Like a rare and tasty wine.

Philippa Sampson

THE RESIDENT

Here is a quiet room
in sunlight.
A radio plays music
softly for Sunday.

Seven grey heads nod randomly,
fourteen hands beat helplessly,
miming lost birds.

As I watch autumn leaves
dappling the window,
I am aware I am not completely
within my own head.

Only the scent of roasting lamb
turns back the clock for me,
and I can remember that home
is another place.

Joyce Harrington

BYGONE DAYS

Lots of fun and mischief
At primary school for me
Going home to Granny's
After school at three

At the age of nine
I went to join my dad
Kuala Lumpur in Malaysia
Life was not so bad

Dad was on the move again
To a place called Kluang
I remember Mum shopping there
At the Kee See Ang

My sister and I off
To boarding school did go.
Midnight feasts, fun and games,
Teachers and matrons shouting
Our names.

A variety of changes were
Happening to me; and yes
I missed going home to
Granny's after school at three.

Ruth McIntyre

ON YOUR OWN

From now on you are
on your own.
To fend for yourself
To get through the worst.

You lie, cheat and steal
Most people want you dead.
You have no friends
And never will.

You destroy anyone,
anyone you get close to.
When they find out
You will be sorry.

Everyone used to like you
To trust you, help you.
But now everyone hates you.
And now you are
                    on your own.

Jennifer Dillon Whitehouse (15)

Bushes And Barley

Little girl
Many years ago
With long nut-brown plaits
Such a serious face and a frown
Sad eyes full of questions

All around her fields and whispering woods
Green country windy and wet
She's lost among the bushes and the barley
Evacuated from the bright lights
Longing for home comforts

Little girl
Many years later
Same long nut-brown plaits
Same serious face and a frown
Sad eyes full of dreams

Of bushes and barley and whispering woods
All around her cars and houses
She's lost in a wilderness of lights
Sheltered from the wind
Longing for adventure

Kersty Strong

LIFE BEGINNING OR JUST ENDING?

When does life begin?
Once conceived or once born?
What was the first feeling ever felt by
        an infant?
What did he understand of life
Setting off, first steps, when?
When is the right time for everyone to
        grow?
To journey through life
From child to toddler, to teens
Who tells him what to feel, to see
        to know?
Through so many feelings of life?
First love, first hurt, new beginnings
Endings, remorse, sadness or happiness
        joy, love.
When does life end or begin?
Can anyone know?

Paula Doyle

ADIEU TRISTESSE

The book unwritten
And the song unsung
And still upon the ladder's lowest rung

When noon takes over
From the dappled morn
The speech unfinished and the child unborn

The hand not offered
And the smile withdrawn
The feeling latent and the moment gone

No task accomplished
And no praises won
Tho' hard the labour in the burning sun

But joys come freely
From the simplest things
The sun's sweet shimmer on butterfly wings

And peace is priceless
And the love of words
Voices of loved ones and the song of birds

Rosemary Coyles

UBIQUITOUS DESTINY

And so she waits,
Clinging onto anticipation that one day will arrive
the inevitable event,
The event that differs from life to life,
differs in all but the final consequence.
The event that throws meaning
on all she has become,
all that has passed,
all that is now,
all that will be.
The event which rewards all hope,
The event that will finally reveal all she is meant to become.
The event that will catapult her out of reality
Into an intoxicating existence of her dreams,
The event that will make the unknown known
Whilst the known becomes a distant memory . . .

And so she waits,
Until her failing eyes see only inwards,
Until in her final seconds she can see
That the event was her life,
Her life was the event,
That she let the event slip away
Whilst waiting for it to happen.

Michelle Pell

LIFE AT THE BUS STOP

Although I see them, at the bus stop every day,
We barely nod in recognition,
In our peculiar British way.
The young man in his charcoal suits,
Calvin Klein jacket, polished Chelsea boots.
Yet, stand too close, and there's the whiff
Of last night's bar,
Stale cigarettes and Stella Artois.

Hurrying along, is the woman in her mac,
The collar turned up, to disguise her latest smack.
She's aware the neighbours hear the rows,
That scream on in the night,
They used to call the police out,
But now, turn out the light.

The old man in the corner house
Waves to the mum next door,
His lungs sound like a squeeze box,
They say he copped it in the war.

The young mum sometimes cooks a meal,
They share a friendly chat,
His beloved wife is gone now
But he won't talk about that.

The little lad is smiling,
As the old man waves bye-bye,
The bus is now approaching,
The air-brakes loudly sigh.

Another cold and windy morning,
But the day is fresh and new,
Man has seven ages,
I observe them in this queue.

Debra Ingram

LAST AUTUMN

The cancer prospers in my father's chest,
His body thins and weakens while it grows
And it is time to face another test.

In living water-colours he expressed
A world his simple tongue could not compose.
The cancer prospers in my father's chest.

At night he drowns in shallow air; distressed,
His heart beats fitfully with feeble blows
And it is time to face another test.

In loving butterflies and birds he best
Captured a freedom only frames enclose.
The cancer prospers in my father's chest.

Today, pain is postponed by drugs and rest,
His voice comes for books on birds, whispers, goes,
And it is time to face another test.

Now, through his window, like a last request,
October paints leaf-pictures at its close.
The cancer prospers in my father's chest
And it is time to face another test.

Geoffrey Mason

ANOTHER CHAPTER
(To Steven, Stephen x 2, Philip, Mark, Thomas and Michael)

I watched them growing
as my son grew
Called them surrogate children
as they invaded my fridge,
my territory.
Suffered the agony
of their acne and first dating
and the waiting
for results
to open doors to further education.

And now as a swarm of locusts
they return
Curtains, steps and goatee beards
and dredlocks for tresses
in hair unwashed for years.
With rings in places
and places for rings
which were never places in my youth,
To pierce a nipple or a navel then
at the very least, uncouth.

Embracing subjects as diverse
as their modish form of dress
Changing course adroitly
with indifference to location.
'Didn't take to engineering
so thought I'd try theology'
From history at St Andrews
to Glasgow for psychology.
Aspirations to a medical or law degree.
Animated noises from deep throaty voices
strangulated in stubbles

Swarming, charming, disarming
Was it only yesterday
my home felt surreptitiously empty?
I retreat to my boudoir,
not needed anymore
and firmly shut the door.

Stephanie Rankin

SECOND CHILDHOOD

I talk to a strange old woman
Who wears my mother's face
From another time she answers
A different voice, a different place,
Inconsequentially.
I repeat myself with careful loudness
Not to be accused of shouting.
I think she knows who I am,
But nothing is certain
In the confused world she inhabits.
Her heart pulses strongly
Her eyes bright as dew in the sunlight
While her mind fades
Into the shadows of night.

J Coyles

OLD TOM

Old Tom resting on the wall by the lych-gate,
Black coat ruffled by the evening breeze;
Idly he watches the lengthening shadows,
Lost in a lifetime of reveries . . .

Slinking in silence through wild graveyard bluebells,
Sifting the scents of a burgeoning spring;
Watching the spiders spin webs by the tombstones,
Waiting to see what the new year might bring . . .

Claws sharp as brambles on midsummer's morning,
Paws soft as moss on the venerable yew;
Eyes cold as marble a-gleam at the sexton,
Hot days asleep on a cool cushioned pew . . .

Damp funeral pyres of leaves in the autumn,
Sweet smelling smoke and the fruits of decay;
Pounce through the mist on a berry-gorged starling,
Feathers and bones mark its passing away . . .

Dining on goose by the inglenook fire,
Christmastide bells ringing carillon-clear;
Licking up cream as the parson sips brandy,
God in His heaven was never so near!

Old Tom resting on the wall by the lych-gate,
Black coat ruffled by the evening breeze;
Idly he watches the lengthening shadows,
Lost in a lifetime of reveries . . .

Alan Hodgson

VEIL

Entirely I adore you,
Discreetly I adore you,
Passionately I adore you.

In the night when I awake,
I find you gone.
I look for someone to embrace,
Where are you?

A lock of hair twists down your face,
Sweet gentle breath waves above.
A gentle perfumed odour,
Sails on the wings of love.

Honeysuckle, apple blossom, lifts the clouds,
Cobwebby curtains, veil you all around.
Sweet peace beholds your face.
A moonbeam carries messages betwixt.
Ripples of the stream are music,
Gentle, oh! So gentle is the songbird.
When midnight arrives my love arriveth too,
And lies beside my bed.
Happiness, sweet happiness is mine,
And all my heart in every corner sings.

Janet Dickson

PARENT POTENTIAL

I'm sure that I would be the best - a natural through and through -
At the finer arts of motherhood and the things that mothers do.
I can feel it all within me, the potential in my heart,
And I'm swotting up from day to day, 'doing the knowledge'
                                                before I start.

When, following months of waiting (and a little push and shove)
I have her bundled in my arms I will tell her of my love.
No matter that she's wrinkled, that her face is red and lined,
I'll wonder at the way she's so exquisitely designed.

The night time feeds that she demands at one o'clock and four,
Will make me smile indulgently as I sweep through her door.
No bleary eyes and swearing, no dark mutterings for me,
I'm sure that I will find short naps are just my cup of tea.

I will rock her gently with one hand and change her with the other,
I will run around non-stop all day then swear she is no bother.
When she grizzles with persistence I'll just be glad that she is fit,
And I'll mash up healthy fruit and veg until she's sick of it.

I will plough through heaps of washing and hold small vests up
                                                to the light,
Then I'll glow with satisfaction that I've washed them up so white.
The line of clothes between the trees will stretch and bow with strain,
'Til I strip it bare and iron the lot and then begin again.

I'll read heaps of books on raising kids to make sure I do things right,
I'll write long lists of do's and don'ts and check them every night.
But the most important thing of all, or so it seems to me,
Is a great big hug three times a day with breakfast, lunch and tea.

Sophie Tucker

EARLY YEARS

When I was born I was very small,
I couldn't sit up, or walk, or crawl.
I hadn't any teeth so I couldn't eat,
and fed from a bottle, through a teat.

As I grew older I used a spoon,
and walked unsteadily round the room.
Teeth grew in my gums so I could eat,
puddings and fish and minced up meat.

Once I could run, my legs grew stronger,
my body grew taller and my arms got longer.
Under my baby teeth my big teeth grew,
and as they fell out my others came through.

I outgrew my clothes and my shoes got too tight,
so I had to have new ones that fitted me right.
I played with my Duplo and rode on my trike,
but now I can balance on a two wheeled bike.

I can eat my dinner with a knife and a fork.
I can read and write, and talk and talk and *talk*.
I used to like Postman Pat, and watch him on TV,
but now it's Superman; he's the hero for me.

I have my hair cut without any fuss,
and help carry shopping when we go on the bus.
My height is on a long chart pinned to the wall.
I'll ride a rollercoaster when I've grown really tall.

Jan Pollard

VICTORY

We all can have a moment, I suppose,
That transubstantiates this common clay;
But much beyond my thought are those
Who scaled far mountain peaks, or trod the way
That leads on through the self to sacrifice;
More simply, those who in a battle died,
Finding a courage reason had denied.

My moment came the other end of time;
I had for summons the deep bell of pain;
Lay in a lonely room, a narrow bed,
And wondered where myself, and nature, led.

My body sucked me down, submerged my will
Into the depths, then cast me up again;
Panting I lay, a sea-thing on the shore,
Then back into the clutch of pain once more,
Fiercer each time, in that long ebb and flow,
Until the final moments, when I drowned,
Dragged down through gulfs of fear and agony.

Then rescue came, for lonely, high,
Broke a new baby's desolating cry.
And then I knew where all my life had led,
Met there the whole of joy and pain for me,
As they held up that tiny, squirming thing,
Bound still to me by a blue, slender thread.

From out my battle, my own kind of strife,
I gave a life.

Lorna Harding

WHEEL OF LIFE

Helpless baby, looking to our mother
for our food, warmth and comfort,
in these early days, there is no other
to supply all our needs and care.
First in a pram, then in a push-chair
before we've learnt to walk alone.
Then to school and lessons, learn to share
and make friends, all the 'ups and downs' of life.
Time to leave school - to work or learn
a trade, profession, now we ride a bike,
proudly to go home, as we can earn
and pay our way at home, with friends.
We're growing up and crave affection,
stolen kisses after dark in cinema
or disco, did we forget to mention
this at home? And kisses in the car.
As time rolls on a mate is sought
for love and marriage, and a family.
The next step a house is bought,
furniture, perhaps a pram for baby.
Many years go by, retirement comes for us,
increasing weakness, an arm or stick
now needed, no more travel by train or bus.
Finally a humbling wheel-chair.
No use to fret about the 'good old days',
we cannot stop the march of time.
'O God please let the end be quick,' each prays
no mournful lingering our loved ones say 'Farewell.'
'A lovely funeral' - to all they'll tell.

Vera Graver

EVOLUTION

Born from darkness into light
Crying out for knowledge,
The apple is eaten,
Wisdom is found
The Devil's then awaiting.
We follow a path that
Suits us best -
Bartering with the Wolf.
A winding path intricately
Takes
    Us through
Unknowing
       Traps.
We come out bold and
Leave the past
Looking ahead for better riches,
But by the time we've found
Our homes,
We experience the darkness.
Hoping that the path once walked
Has led us into heaven.

Abhilasha Masih

CHILD OF MINE

Child of mine, you light my day
Whilst in your bed you quietly lay,
Remembering first days of feat
Unsteady times upon your feet.

First mumbled words and cheeky smile
That make your tantrums seem worthwhile,
Fair locks that crowd upon your face
Each curl hung within its place.

Moments filled with childish laughter
Stories ending, happily ever after,
Knowing when to start the tears
To get your way, these fast flown years.

Eyes of wonderment and glee
Of many treasures yet to see,
You fill my life with endless joy
Child of mine, amongst your toys.

Maria Colvin

LIFE FROM START TO FINISH

First you come screaming into the world frightened and useless,
Then you learn how to walk and talk, think and do,
Then it is your time to make decisions about how you want to
live your life,
And then you are old, unable to do much that you did before,
and then you are dead and gone.
As you were before your beginning so you are now after your
end unless . . . ?

H R Laden

UNTITLED

My hands in front of me
I seem contained, somehow
concealing the empty space
in the circle of my arms.
I hold on for my own dear life
in a girl gesture
that helps me chameleon,
so no-one should see or seize me
and no-one will love and leave me.

Sarah-Jane Wren

TIME SAVERS

When man started forth in this world of ours
There was nothing to help him to do all the chores.
He first drank from shells, then invented the cup,
Then he invented the prop to hold his wash up.
Other gadgets soon followed to ease his lifestyle,
Not forgetting the glass, to make drinking worthwhile.

He first fought with stones, before inventing the bow,
Then along came the wheel, his weapons to tow.
With this he made clocks to tell him the time,
And a bike to ride on; oh! Life was just fine.
The wheel proved it was the best invention so far,
It wasn't so long before man had his first car.

He invented the beer, then invented the tap,
He invented the mug for knocking it back.
Machines were then thought of to do the week's wash,
Along with the dryer, to make them feel posh.
The typewriter came next, so they could write faster;
It all added up, to save time for the master.

Steam engines, once thought the best to save time,
Were succeeded by tractors, now the farmers felt fine.
There were plenty of gadgets, all thought to be winners,
Like the microwave oven, to save time for the dinners.
All these are time savers? Not on your nellie -
So just to even things up, they invented the telly!

Sidney Talbot

YOUTH

Youth is like a sickness,
that passes with time.
Youth teaches us to show emotion,
is a weakness, and a crime.
We are cheats, and liars,
nothing we say is sincere.
We build walls to keep people away,
no one must come near.
Good times come before lovers,
no thought of commitment in our mind.
Youth teaches us so many ways to be unkind.

M A Challis

MEMORIES

Now that I am heavy with years,
And my hands lie still on my knees,
I sit in my parlour window
In the waft of the balmy breeze,
And I think of the primrose and
        violet
In the woods at the end of the lane
The bluebells a carpet of heaven
As they were on the day you came.

Now that I am heavy with years,
And my days of toil are done,
I sit in my parlour window
In the blaze of the summer sun,
And I know that my roses are blooming
By the sweet incoming scent,
And the lavender's high at the gate
As it was on the day you went.

M Richards

ENTRANCES AND EXITS

When I was just a little girl
I thought I'd like to knit.
I learnt to plain, I learnt to purl
But sadly, that was it.

I went to junior school, of course,
It took some years to strike me
That I got teased so much because
They really didn't like me.

A very new and nervous wife
I did what Arnold said,
But nothing ever came to life
When we two went to bed.

The middle years just disappeared
Our hopes all fizzled out.
We somehow got the children reared
While we ourselves got stout.

The Granny time is not at all
What it's cracked up to be!
I got quite tired of bat and ball
And 'Nana, look at me!'

Old women tend to leak and smell,
I'm sorry for my daughter
And if she doesn't treat me well
It must be how I taught her.

The doctor thinks I cannot hear
His smile says it's alright,
But I can read him loud and clear:
I'm going to die tonight.

Ursula Kiernan

AN AGE OF 'ISMS'

Born as a bare slate,
A clean page in a heavy volume called life,
no sense of being, thrown to nature or is it nurture.

Those pre-school, ever so important years,
when one's person is woven so intrinsically,
to follow us all our days.
Ageism, sexism, racism, feminism,
take your pick 'ism'.

One trauma follows another in the book of life.
Enter school with yet more stereotypes,
bullies, pretty faces, bright minds,
Intimidation a silent inward pain.

By now if one succeeds you enter your working years.
Satisfaction replaced by despondency,
reality sets in it's just a job.

The relationship stage rears its head,
a flush of hormones off to bed.
Family, work, guilt, more 'isms',
A large G & T will see it through.

Retirement drags its feet in,
but one hasn't the energy to give it a good run.
Self exploration, finding oneself.
There's sure to be an 'ism' about.

And finally if one survives to those latter twilight days,
You may be surplus to requirements.
An old folk's home full of rules, limiting and ageist.
But that's if you're lucky,
Euthanasia might be knocking at your door.

Kathleen Byrne

STONE CIRCLES

From stone circles past to St Paul's great dome
From the age of bronze to our age of chrome
Man has carved and created, demolished and grasped
With wit and wisdom, blood letting flint axe
Many times in vain many times alone
In equatorial or temperate zone
They've knelt in prayer or they've been dispatched
From stone circles past
They followed instinct and challenged the known
Pushing back frontiers from the first seeds sown
Pursuing ideals creating new tracks
Striding out zealous embracing the task
Unearthing the new along with old bones
From stone circles past.

Michael Bigland

THE INNOCENT CHILD

What happened to those innocent eyes
Of the naked babe
Who on the sheepskin lies
In the photograph on the mantelshelf.

Innocence clutched her satchel to school
With a confidence
To understand the rule
To work, to play to succeed, to obey.

Eleven plus to the telling years,
Guarding innocence,
Examination fears
Of failure intending to wreck the plan.

Then unfolding like a scene untaught
A new pulse shyly
Sparked radiance and brought
Flattery, so ardently in its fire.

Blindly through portals of the nave came
Innocence sublime,
Changing not just the name,
Challenge of emotions to be defined.

Travelling wide the family years
Patterned with desires
And hopes that potent fears
Of broken dreams would die unrealised.

Don't be deceived by those fading eyes,
She's not infantile,
But still the same in guise
Of wisdom, learned by the innocent child.

Jill Willens

THE PLUM TREE

She weeps her snow
in a silken drift
like a loss mourned,
like a maiden's shift
loosened, fallen
around her feet.
Seduced by the sun
her pain is sweet,
deflowered by thrust
of summer come
she waits to swell
with succulent plum.

Chris Moat

ABOUT MOTHERS

When God without our aid fulfilled creation's plan
He then a mother made and helper for her man.
And there he hid beneath her wing,
A recompense
For suffering!

A faithful friend is she be it in gain or loss
But stands in constancy at cradle, bench or cross.
A tower strong who chose ere long
In mind and heart,
That better part.

For hands that held the rein; and lips that spoke of grace'
For eyes that smiled through pain; a loving mother's face.
Her children rise and to the skies
Her love confess
Her soul to bless!

When God who reigns above in perfect deity
Had set on earth in love the human family;
Then was it thus that he for us
Adorned with grace,
A mother's face?

M Fisher-Obren

Spirit Of The Rainforest

From beyond the fronds he peered face as the tiger stripes he wore,
Merging with nature's shades of green while all around the forest
                                        gave of its sounds,
Native of this forest in which he lives the sounds and sights within
                                        his heart,

Multicoloured birds interweave the trees on a high chase game
                                        of courtship,
Screeching monkeys from high branches swing like trapeze
                                        artists swift and sure,
Nature at her glorious best wonders at her feet and in the air,

He fears not of the tiger with its killer instinct but of man with
                                        the instinct to kill,
Greed the disease and the destruction rife at the fingertips,
The elders the danger have long known the perils to befall upon this
                                        planet,

Stripping away the heart of the trees making sparse the vegetation,
In the name of progress, warning had passed on from the
                                        generation before,
This he had learned heavy his anguish diminished his spirit,

Living the very essence of life spiritual in harmony in this world,
Nature is fighting back on their behalf, this boy born of the forest,
Which in him lives and breathes whose earth is at his very pulse,

Receives back more joy than modern man could ever know,
One day the planet will be back to basics stripped bare a barren land,
From the embers life on earth will bring forth a new generation
                                        who will listen,

They will see the wisdom all around living in simplicity in harmony
with creation,
As it comes into fruition, for now he enraptures at the delights
that abound,
Nature sustaining life in turn respecting nature free for all and all
for free,

The fronds closing in as the face disappears.

Ann G Wallace

SUMMER REP, NORTH: 1951

I climbed the stairway - Programme? - Certainly -
     Let's see who's in the cast tonight - (Quite pretty
That serving-wench - spoken for, more's the pity,
     So just a walk-on here, for her and me!)

The play's the thing, they say; and I'm quite certain
     My role's a minor one - no room for airs,
Feuds, tantrums - while the back-stage love-affairs
     Die off, unwept, behind the final curtain.

But somehow I've ad-libbed, and it has passed,
     The stage-fright, costumes, grease-paint, strident light;
The SM drops the tabs on us; the cast
     Disperse into that other world: it's night.

I asked a playbill and was given grief,
     Delight, fear, hope - the gamut: but up there,
Offering the programme for my mortal life
     She stands yet, at the summit of the stair.

John E Cunningham

NEW-BORN

Her soul I sensed
whose pristine innocence
and goodness, seemed
to recognised our bond
and know its peace
and whence it came, as she
of waxen warmth
so recently new-born -

Her radiant smile
said trust as I do you
and I shall grow
and blossom in my time
to share this bond
so firmly held in Him
who placed me small
and helpless in your arms -

Yet chosen, called
to bud and branch His vine,
and bear much fruit
that He will gather up
He blessed in His
to make new wine
for that great harvest feast
He longs to share
one day in love sublime.

Rosemary Keith

CHILDHOOD ASTRAL

Rising up
on your night journey
joy and terror
mingling
to enter that
strange landscape
where dreams
come true
to cross the threshold
into dark forests
softness
softness breathes the night

and always
the terrible fear
of being alone
and separate
of not getting back
in again
of losing the day
to the beauty of the night.

Julian Ronay

A LIFESPAN

The world is like a giant stage
Which we enter at an early age
As an infant . . . helpless but alive
Dependant on an adult to survive.

Childhood comes onto the scene
Where great development is seen.
But now the troubled teenage years
Growing up through the traumas, joys and tears.

Then on to early adulthood
When some settle down to produce a brood.
The twenties and the thirties too
Are the best years of your life, that's true.

When the forties and the fifties come
A lot of excess baggage gathers round the tum,
The teeth and hair and eyes are changing
A lot of bits need re-arranging.

Now comes the age of real maturity
Of concessionary rates and reduced ability.
From the age of sixty on
A lot of the body's elasticity's gone.

There's the sagging boobs and the sagging bum
But if you think that's bad . . . there's even worse to come . . .

As now you are at the geriatric age
Where you get the rest of the symptoms of old age.
Creaking joints and aches and pains
Hardening of the arteries and softening of the brains.

By the time you're an octogenarian
You have nearly completed the master plan.
Helpless and dependant in your second childhood
Just awaiting to retire from the stage, for good.

Mary Anne Scott

THE BIRTHDAY PARTY

Here journeys intersect,
Converging at dependency:
One coming, one going -
Briefly side by side.

A commonality found
In servants, dribbled food,
Incontinence.

Toothless and burbling,
They share a secret language;
Exchange enigmatic smiles.

Patrick B Osada

SEVEN STAGES

First a babe in his mother's arms
Looking with pleasure at all her charms.

Walking by a school child, wishing all the while.

A lover blissful in earnest, gently takes cover.

A soldier though he looks no older.

Then a little larger with a belly to match.

Now spectacle on nose he prefers a little poise.

So now a little older, can see and sense once more.

Wendy Barber

HUMAN RACE

Think how far mankind has come,
since he first stood up to run.
He travels now the speed of sound
and flies the world all around.
He races on in big fast cars
and launches rockets to the stars.
He speeds around from dawn till dusk
in his quest to earn a crust.
And lives his life at such a pace,
he'll soon out-run the human race.
And when at last his days are done
he'll find he's not had any fun.
He's had no time to stop and stare
or had any time to really care
for others who have in their turn
raced and chased their wage to earn.
So what is left of Eden then,
that beautiful garden, peaceful glen.
Well, it's bleak, it's sparse and full of trash,
for man has sold it all for cash.

Daphne E Cornell

BEACH FOOTBALL

'Play on!' junior ref commands
run, jump, attack, defend
so glories arise on level sand
from frantic sport played end to end
skills performed with zeal and zest
and 'bags that I be Georgie Best.'

Between folded coats they make their mark
but the glory boys will be denied
by a counter offensive after dark
and a rising swell from deep offside
time and tide's inevitable creep
sweeps the beach while opponents sleep.

'Watch this, dad!' skills displayed
polished, honed, relayed
and to this moment they belong
where mad dogs gad and grey waves crash
till autumn lighting fades
on two generations at their song.

On Bridlington front
where it's nice to get out if you can
they'll turn on benches and say
it was different in my day
now banner headlines shout the score
'Striker says, 'I'll quit'
and the Yorkshire Belle sets sail
determined in her way
then fading in the bay.

John Clarke

A HUMDRUM LIFE

Reminiscing is a game
We oldies play, to pass the time:
Perhaps we bore those near and dear,
But self-indulgence is no crime!

The nursery days are far away:
Such cherished care where love abounds;
And all around one, comfort glows;
No discord, stress, or ugly sounds.

When school begins, you feel the jolt
Of strangers in your life; but fast
You learn to give and take,
Forget the coddling of the past.

Then next, those happy carefree days,
When love and romance rule your world;
You never pause to stop and think,
When round the ballroom floor you're whirled.

Marriage and children follow that:
Fulfilment? Yes, but times are hard
When small one's needs predominate;
So luxuries for oneself are barred.

Now comes a spell of peace and quiet;
Because the kids are moving on,
You take up hobbies, new pursuits;
And wonder where the years have gone.

So, there you have my humdrum life!
The secret bits are locked away;
They're far too precious to divulge:
You'll never know; I'll never say.

Corinne Lovell

WILL YOU?

Will you walk with me through springtime
And will you talk with me about life's epic journey
Together we have promised one another?

Will you run with me through sunlit summer days
And will you love with me so all our hours are filled
With happiness?

Will you stroll with me through autumn's misty loveliness
And will you hold my hand when winter day turns
Into cruel night?

Will you pray with me when like a candle flame
Life flickers out
And will you say goodbye?

Philip W Utridge

IMMATURITY

A certain unripe condition
Which causes us to fail?
An unfortunate rendition
With all it can entail . . .
Is that immaturity?

Slip? Make mistakes, indeed don't all?
Imperfect we are made.
We stumble others, sometimes fall,
Oft times we ask for aid . . .
Is that immaturity?

No stumbling tongue, no way transgress,
Offence never to give,
Wisdom on all to firm impress,
Can I to this rule live . . .
Perfect in maturity?

Alas! We all expect too much
From our associates.
When it's not there we tend to blame
Not self, but other's traits.
Whose is immaturity?

Evelyn Balmain

DISCOVERING STILL

At seventy-three, I should have thought
That life held few surprises;
That I had seen and heard and known
Nature in all her guises.

But as I watch, I notice now
New tricks of light and shadow,
A way the wind moves in the leaves,
A difference in the rainbow.

As I re-read some well-loved lines
New meaning I discover,
And music blossoms in my mind
That once I had passed over.

And you my friends - we've talked and laughed
So many times together -
The true companions of my heart
In every kind of weather.

Yet still, as time goes by, you show
New traits, gifts unsuspected,
And so you speak and act in ways
I never had expected.

Knowledge is ringed with mystery
In this life, short and fleeting,
And we must say farewell so soon
To those we have been greeting.

All knowledge and all mystery
Proceed from God alone,
And when we reach His world of light,
We'll know as we are known.

Sheila Durbin

VALENTINE'S DAY

When I was young and in my prime
I always received a Valentine.
'Twas intrigue, mystery and fun
To think that somebody's heart I'd won.

And as the days went rolling by
The culprit didn't seem so shy.
Out into the open he began to move,
And there and then declared his love!

We married then one Saturday morn,
Lived happily together through sunshine and storm,
Until one day he passed away.
Well now there's nothing left to say!

Dorothy Lloyd

NEW MILLENNIUM MAN

When man appeared who could foretell
If it was going to augur well,
Who could foresee the more he learned
The more his fingers would be burned.
Yet progress had to play its part
And so he came with trembling heart,
To occupy his present site
But guilty of more wrong than right.
Now, lord of all that he surveys
He's tried in vain so many ways,
To bring about true peace on earth
Since his conception and his birth.
But so far this elusive state
Time after time has had to wait,
He finds it very hard to do
To make man's dearest wish come true.
But now he's looking through a door
Which simply wasn't there before,
He sees a new millennium rise
Over twenty first century's skies.
Now is his chance to make amends
Helping enemies to be friends,
And he beholds a golden age
The turning of another page,
Of man's turbulent history
While pondering what is to be,
He wonders if true peace will reign
After long centuries of pain.
New millennium man must be
The architect of harmony.

Moira Wiggins

THE THING IN THE CHAIR

What's that there, the thing in the chair?
Where? Oh that! It's there so often, I've
Forgotten about it -
Just go round it, it won't bother you -
We usually ignore it.

It made a noise you say? Really?
Is it in your way?
We'll pretend it isn't there, the thing in the chair.
It's harmless, quiet, we never let it intrude into
Our busy, exciting lives.

Bye for now, see you at the party next week.
What's that you say? The thing seems to leak -
Tiny wet droplets spill silently from the chair.
So near a tear;
Too unaware to care . . .

. . Hello! You missed the party - We missed you.
Where were you? - I say - A funeral that day!
Anyone we know? You wouldn't think so
Yes, we'd love to visit this evening, late,
For another party date -
See you!

Come in, welcome to an evening of laughter and chat -
What's that you're staring at?
The thing over there;
An old *empty* chair
Suddenly the whole room seems bare.

'Cept for *that* chair
We were too busy to care,
Yet *she* was always there . . .

. . . And we never said goodbye.

See you around!

(Anyone want a chair?)
Free!

Pam Phillips

MEMORY

Ride little rocking horse,
Into the past,
Backwards not forwards,
Into the past.

Ride little rocking horse,
Into the past,
Backwards not forwards,
Make the ride last.

Ride little rocking horse,
And as you go,
Backwards not forwards,
What do you know?

Ride on, ride on,
Tell us your song,
Backwards not forwards,
Was the road long?

Ride little rocking horse,
Were you ever afraid,
Backwards not forwards,
I'll bet you were brave!

Oh, little rocking horse,
Riding so fast,
Into the past,
Into the past.

Oh, little rocking horse,
Wait for me,
Have you forgotten,
I was only three.

Netta P Mills

THE SEASONS: FALL

My world has closed around me
Like a hoop, fast cooling on a cask.
I have become bound, confined.
Unable now to move too far,
I keep my treasures close,
Within an arm's length of this chair,
And take delight in simple things.
The gas fire on a darkening day,
The cold light of the morning:
The deep intrusions of the lowering sun,
Finding out the furthest reaches of this room.

Twice a week the cleaner comes, busy, distant, bustling:
Telling of holidays, hotels, exotic meals
And brandishing snaps of faraway lands.
I gaze past her, at the tree beyond my window.
These sixty years I've watched it grow
And yet I do not know it: it surprises me still.

Terry Sweetman

HE TRIED

Now I'll tell you the story of a man who couldn't win,
He worked so hard, he persevered, he fought through thick and thin,
Despite his best endeavours he didn't reach the summit,
More than once he slipped right back just when he thought
                                                       he'd done it.
But he tried.

When George was born - an only child - his parents had ambitions,
They saw their son a great success, ensconced in high positions,
And while at school he studied well to meet their expectations,
The trouble was he found it hard to pass examinations.
But he tried.

When war broke out in '39 he joined up with the rest,
He had no stomach for the fight although he did his best,
He learned to be a soldier and prepared himself for action,
Applied for a commission, failed selection by a fraction.
But he tried.

For forty years he slaved away against great competition,
With regular promotion he was fired with fresh ambition,
The top jobs were within his grasp, he'd realised his potential,
His face, however, didn't fit - of course that was essential.
But he tried.

In later years, George tried his hand at musical composing,
He thought he'd write a hit or two, he found the work engrossing,
He sent his songs to publishers, his lyrics were quite clever,
Rejection slips came thick and fast - his name was *not* Lloyd Webber.
But he tried.

At last his long and happy life came to a peaceful end,
And those he left behind him really felt they'd lost a friend,
To various relations he bequeathed his small estate,
He would have taken it with him but he left it far too late.
'Though he tried.
How he tried.'

George Main

BARE

When penning prose, one has to suppose,
A soul is laid to bare.
Through glimpsing life, of joys and strife,
That, so openly we share.

Hopes and dreams and aspirations,
Honest, brutal and true,
Etched forever in mind, on paper,
An epitaph to you.

Mundane, exciting, earnest, serene,
An emotional rotating sphere,
Absorbing, deleting, embracing life
A vehicle, hard to steer.

As complex, yet as ordinary
Vast experience shows.
A chequered past, a colourful life,
The book we one day close.

Carolyn Boylan

REMEMBERING CHILDHOOD

When days were full of sunshine,
The laughter came with ease,
How great the age of innocence,
When the moon was made of cheese.

In dreams we would see Santa,
Or wish upon a star,
And place teeth under pillows,
For the fairy from afar.

Streets were safe, we knew not fear,
There was no cause to fret,
No responsibility,
No overwhelming debt.

We'd never heard of drug abuse,
Nor seen a gun or knife,
How sad we grow up all too soon,
To face the real life.

How much worse must it become,
Before we change our ways,
And give our children half a chance,
To remember happy days.

Julie Wright

A SUSSEX VILLAGE AT WAR

We grimly listened as our leader spoke of war declared,
And in the months which followed actively prepared
For the invasion which, thank God, was not to be,
Our island fortress girt around by priceless sea.

We proudly watched from vantage points in lane and field
As Hitler's aerial hordes were trounced above the Sussex Weald.
We gratefully saluted those brave boys in blue,
For ne'er before was so much owed to men so few.

We laboured hard to wrest an increase from the soil,
To 'Dig for Victory' was our aim, our constant toil.
Allotments sprang from fields where erstwhile cows had been,
And vegetables replaced the former lawns of green.

We gave our cash to keep our servicemen equipped,
Thereby ensuring that our deadly foe was whipped.
With special 'Weeks' to save for ships and planes and arms,
We tried our best to shield our 'boys' from war's alarms.

We kept our nerve when news was bad and spirits fell.
Morale was boosted in too many ways to tell.
Collectively we vowed to never bend the knee:
To settle for nought else than final victory.

At last the great day dawned, our freedom was assured:
Our gallant lads returned for well-deserved reward.
We mourn the twenty-five who we shall see no more,
For they have given their all - a sacrifice to war.

And now a new dawn bids us go ahead once more,
A village now more closely knit that e'er before.
Six years of combined wartime efforts now must cease,
But may the unity achieved therein now win the peace.

John Eldridge

The Seven Ages Of Music

My piano lessons began at the age of four
I was really too young, practice seemed like a bore.
Eventually I managed to pass my Grade Two,
But enough was enough and I sought interests new.

In my teenager years how I wished I could play,
A good teacher was found, that is all I will say.
He didn't last long, I had to go to college,
How I wished that I had more musical knowledge.

I had to go in search of teacher number three,
Who eventually made a good pianist of me.
I loved teaching kids songs and recorders as well,
You could say I was under music's magic spell.

My grandfather's violin was one hundred years old,
A copy of Jacobus Stainer I was told.
I started with lessons, began scraping away,
Not so good as piano, but interesting to play.

My career as a teacher was nearing its end,
'Why don't you join the church choir?' suggested a friend.
I plucked up my courage and did as she had said,
I sing at services and when couples are wed.

Retirement meant time spent on harmony lessons,
How I enjoyed these lively creative sessions.
In a local orchestra I started to play,
How exciting, I thought, it's really made my day.

To play a church organ was my next ambition,
To master the pedals is my present mission.
I pull out the stops as a voluntary I play,
P'raps I'll play for a service at some future day!

Heather Middleton

THE RACE OF TIME

Time accelerates so quickly,
Months and years go flashing by.
Birthdays come and go so swiftly
you could almost sit and cry.
It's no use sitting down to mope,
Or crying wasteful tears.
It's not the years in life that count,
But the life that's in your years.

Brian O'Brien

REAL LOVE?

I don't know how to tell you,
I don't know how you'll feel,
When I say I love you,
I know this love is real.

I don't know how you'll take it,
When I say forever,
I know I'll love you always,
I want us to be together.

I don't know if you like me,
Never mind us getting married,
It's just a dream not reality,
A burden I've always carried.

I need to say I want you,
That I have done all my life,
But I know nothing will come of it,
As it'll just cause lots of strife.

Allison Woodhead

BY THE GATE

Standing in the feeling
of early spring,
with unaccustomed warmth
fingering your silvered hair,
you watch forsythia
burst slowly,
and long shadows shorten.
Is it still amazing
that this created beauty
is ours, for the opening
of a door?

Linda Williams

IN THE ABSENCE OF HOPE

The mood I woke up in today
Embraces my life
In many aspects
I want much more out of life
Then I already have
What I have is nothing
I wanted to end my life
Nothing is going my way
Nothing is happening as I want it
I have many dreams
That remain unfulfilled
In the absence of hope
I carry on dreaming
In my subservient position.

Kauser Parveen

CHRISTMAS-MOODY PEOPLE

Daring shop-window displays, and lights hung aloft
Made children hanker for Christmas, and plead with mean
Parents, to bring decorations out of the loft.

Carol-cassettes and CDs on the stereo
Sets in department stores serenaded adults,
Killing their 'sensible' blues, with capriccio.
No longer do queues by grottos seem insults
To their collective, less credulous ego.

That's the beginning of Christmas-disease. Folk start
Haggling with market traders for decent trees
At bargain-basement costs - and new sets of lights,
So they can throw their old lots in the dustman's cart.
'These sort don't blow fuses. Take it from me!'

Gillian C Fisher

TEA AND BISCUITS

'He's reached a crisis stage,' they said
Thinking I was too far gone to understand
Then went out for their tea break
Leaving me on the machine
With pipes to feed me
And him they hadn't seen
Grinning at the foot of the bed.
'I was there at your first crisis stage,'
He smirked, 'When you were three
And fell off your trike.
And then when Fiona
Proved faithless and you
Stood on the supermarket roof
And threatened to jump.
And then . . . '
The alarm went off.
Beep . . . Beep . . . Beep . . .
'Hell fire,' he cried
'That's my parking meter run out'
And ran out.
'What the devil?' they cried
Running in. Then laughed
And said 'Why, it's just his
Getting better alarm.'
Then they tucked me in and said
'You'll want something solid now
Nothing fanciful mind.'
'Tea and biscuits please,' I said.

Brian Evans

FAST FORWARD!

Technology has now taken over
Computers and micro-chips
All thoughts they do slip
Man has no power
While machines come to tower
Buildings grow high
They come close to the sky
Just the press of a button
Takes control of our lives
The remote control has arrived
We look to our screens
We seek all it beams
Transmissions and admissions
Our thoughts and our minds
With machines, they entwine
But life is not what it seems
Taking all nature
We have entered a new future
A world full of walls
Electronically well fitted
Secured and uplifted
We are no longer gifted
Mother nature we have shifted.

Suzan Gumush

THE SEVEN AGES OF A MODERN HUMAN

All the world's a virtual theatre,
And all the men and women merely cyber-actors;
They have their relationships and inter-personal dynamics,
And each person in their time plays many roles,
Their acts being seven ages.
At first the lone-parent child,
Bought up on benefit in an extended family.
Then the school-kid,
With overloaded satchel and National Curriculum,
Roller-blading to a grant-maintained Portakabin.
And then the student, with pockets empty,
Working for a degree amidst socialising,
When it will not even guarantee a job.
Then the lover, searching for a life partner,
Through the minefield of dinner parties,
Looking at furniture every weekend.
Then terrible middle-age.
Where you have to be wise and experienced,
Yet strive to be trendy enough,
To avoid embarrassing your children.
The next age is no rose-tinted retirement,
With pitiful golden handshake for life's long toil,
And a meagre pension to fall back on.
Last scene of all,
A dingy retirement home,
Confused and longing for visitors,
Or something interesting to happen.
Sans money, sans dignity . . . sod everything!

Andrew Fisher

NEVER ENDING QUEST

For more knowledge man will seek
Another mountain, another peak
Deep ocean beds he's longed to go
To see the wonders down below.

To walk another planet's face
Only Earth once man did grace
In his mind for centuries past
His knowledge widened, men learned fast.

As time went by his thoughts they grew
He and others slowly flew
How his rate of learning has grown
To distant planets he has flown.

He's climbed the highest mountain peak
Through the airways he now speaks
He knew one day he would go
Deep below to see the show.

In time to come our planet dead
Out there somewhere inside man's head
Another mountain peak
Another ocean bed.

Roy Taylor

THE TIME OF ALONE

I take your hand, past the
circus dweller, to see a
solitary man - where restless imagination
imagines countless complication and
this: sour screams and
gnashing thoughts and
bloody cuts gaping raw
where maggots suck and maggots crawl
in a vapour alone.
'Tell him' - tell him to wait to
wrestle for sanity but you can't,
you never saw.
'You' never saw where
just the basic has fled and
nothing's left - insanity.

Dave Bronn

REFLECTIONS ON LIFE AS WE APPROACH THE MILLENNIUM

'The millennium looms in sight,
And all we can worry about is computer blight!
When the world is full of sadness - a sorry old state,
If we don't wake up soon it will be too late.
CJD disease is amongst us and violence abounds,
So many roads being built - we'll soon run out of ground.
Why don't we address the problems of unemployment, aggression
                                            and addiction,
That has led to the mindless desecration of the Sacred Sites of
                                            our nation?
Manifest in graffiti on stones at Avebury, white pain on St Michael's
                                            Tower at Glastonbury,
Smashed stones on the Yorkshire Moors and red paint on the White
                                            horse at Westbury.
Politicians seem to ignore this and few people seem to care
About this beautiful countryside that we all share.
Please wake up soon before it's too late,
And look back to the past to stop this terrible fate,
That will be our legacy to our children if we don't make a stand,
And work with Mother Earth manifest as Nature, hand in hand.
Look back to the wisdom of the ancient tribes,
Who held Mother Earth as sacred as she provided all they needed
                                            to stay alive.
Teach respect for Mother Earth and reverence for the Sacred Sites,
Care for her people, plants and animals to make the balance right.
Search for the Divine Spark that exists within
That connects me to you and you to him.
For all is one and one is all upon this Earth,
So think before acting so as not to create a dearth.
Our greed and desire for material gain
Has caused Mother Earth great pain.
The balance must be redressed before it's too late,
So instead of moping and bemoaning your fate,
Take care what you buy, use and throw away.

Act now - no time to lose - I mean today.
If we all act now and stick to this plan,
Mother Earth will renew and continue to give pleasure to man.
But if we carry on in this careless, mindless way,
All could be lost and no future left for our children one day.
Bring back love and compassion to stop the spirit of sadness
That stalks our land and replace it with a spirit of gladness.
Prepare now and regard the Millennium as a new start,
In which we can all play our part,
By sowing the seeds for a new golden age,
Bringing joy and peace - not road rage!'

J A Marshall

OLD MEN'S HOME

Carpet-footed for a long day
all day through the same day
trudging back again tomorrow.

> Give a ghost up,
> ghost of getting out again!
> (tomorrow it will be
> maybe; or after tea)

Tonight
a clock strikes; and quietly come the old grave men
slippered, and slowly counting
one . . . two . . . three . . . go! No
four . . . five . . . five . . . they're not
by any rule alive;
and the grey hand over faces passes
quarters, halves, hours, in solemn round.

The great brown dog
creeping sideways through the shifting fears
that walk the flat low winter
is a wind of barking, a grave
growling in the ground's throat;
the shadow prowling
is the sliding ways of years.

Old man,
bare the shoulder in your coat!
The thistle will be needle to the coming dark . . .
fog of your age, the anaesthetic: take it
as you would a splinter in the gristle.
Only gently, before your tongue has dried,
whistle for the brown dog
to wear you at his servant side.

Roland Portchmouth

JOURNEY'S END

A time when all is done.
No laughter left - no fun.
No joy remains, or tears.
No sorrow now, or fears.

No thoughts, or need to cry.
One tender word 'Goodbye'
Whispered in memory,
Of how life used to be.

Love shared between these two.
Companions all life through.
But now these ties must break,
One heart alone will ache.

Time alone for them to pray,
Just to meet again some day.
To live a life as full as this,
A gentle touch, a fleeting kiss.

All movement stops - the final breath,
Eternal life? Or simply *death*.

Norman Brookes

FROM THE MOUNTAINS DOWN TO THE SEA

High within the mountains of infancy,
the trickle of a river began its life.
It stumbled and tumbled within stony culverts,
and more than once faltered in its pace.

Slowly, with gentle strength arising,
the trickle became a gushing stream.
Its own momentum carried along, the
course of a life to be foretold.

But suddenly, and before I realised,
the stream had become a roaring river.
Seeking violently burst its boundary
and to drown all within its reach.

Flash floods plagued this aqueous road,
as it tore blindly through the landscape.
Falling in, you would be swept away, and
lucky to be cast upon the bank, alive.

But then, from beyond the distant horizon,
the presence of the sea is felt.
Its weight a prelude to another current,
the turning tide to another life.

For now my river is deep and clear,
the energy of youth is spent, and left
far behind. Whilst ever broadening,
the river becomes an estuary,
a doorway to the open sea.

Where one life ends, and another begins.

Peter Barrett

DAYS OF YOUTH

Strange the things we remember -
The childhood dreams we had,
They flutter in and out our minds
Some are happy, some are sad.

We dream of running with our friends
In golden fields of corn,
But childhood dreams are shattered -
And the adult world is born.

Andrea Hayes

OUT OF SIGHT, OUT OF . . .

Children skipping,
Singing dashing through the streets,
Awaking from winter's slumber,
Spring emerges,

Birds flirting in the slates,
Darting, weaving,
The young boy's kite imaginary enemy deceiving,

Sky breaking blue with clouds of cotton,
In mid day hue,
Buds breaking through,
Flowers shyly peeping from shelters of green,

Women shaking sheets,
Beating mats,
Sending fright to ginger tom,
Catching spring's midday sun,

Store keepers opening doors,
Quarry workers shedding capes,
A child breaking free mother's strings,
Dashing tumbling into nature's bloom,

A grey squirrel rolls dead unnoticed to the side of the road,
Leaving no dent on the speeding van,

The girl's hopeless confused sobs rack her fragile frame
Tampered and withered she lays,
Her father's words of love still echoing around her head.

P D Taylor

TECHNOLOGICAL EROSION

The old flat iron, a door stop, the cauldron replete with blooms,
Now externally displayed, beneath the home's plastic glazed rooms.
Once utensils of the kitchen, until progressions misfortune,
Moderated once their status, including the besom broom.

Long lost the treadle's harmonies, when stitching with exertion.
The cast iron wheel no longer turns, encased in time's corrosion.
Its residue, a work bench, for the electric lathe there upon.
Elapsed the art of needlecraft, via progressions transformation.

The horse brass, ornamental trophies worthy of the shire,
Redundantly embellish, oak surrounds, where once a fire.
As heating pipes engrossed the walls, the coal house need, expired,
Now homage for the freezers, until no longer they're required.

From the scythe to combine-harvester, may be machines that fly,
Sucking the crop from growing roots, by computer memory drive.
Life's consequence seems fatal, should it be so modified;
Eradicating general knowledge, if of this, we were deprived.

Sara Russell, Golden Eagles MCC

WHEN?

When will the thirst of barren lands
be quenched?
When will the fire of man's inhumanity
be drenched?
When will hostilities between the nations
cease?
When will the starving millions ever know
release?
When will the fountains of greed and hatred
end?
When will the broken-hearted find their hearts
will mend?

When the final trumpet sounds
that's when!
When the Lord rides out of heaven
with awesome angels by His side!
When His glory fills the sky
and His name is lifted high,
that's when!

Oceans will thunder their welcome;
in reverence, the mountains will bow;
great deserts will burst into new life.
The creation, adoring His name.

The deaf will hear;
the blind will see;
the lame will jump for joy,

and those who've long awaited Him,
will gaze, in rapture, on His face!

Hilary Philips

WHEN DID WE BECOME OLD?

I watch you shuffling
I know I shuffle too!
But I feel the same as when I married you!
You had lovely hair then
And you had muscles too.
You used to pick me up and swing me around
And whisper 'I love you.'
Oh, I know that you still love me
But it's all so different now
We've become so used to each other
It's not the same somehow
And yet we're still the lovers
Who married so long ago
And we have lived a full life,
Not always free from woe
As we stroll towards our fiftieth
I can look back and say
I'm glad that we're together
On this our golden day.

Joan E Bartlett

WE PASS THROUGH THIS WORLD BUT ONCE

All naked and pale looking we are born
so helpless but with a very loud horn.
By screaming we make contact
it seems all so perfect.

As we cry due to frights
our parents have sleepless nights.
Soon we can images identify
if it's mum or dad we can verify.

We gurgle and giggle
and always wiggle
and sometimes waggle
to the sound of the rattle.

Soon we are on our feet
and ready for any feat
at school we are a menace
with teachers looking for solace.

In no time with a girl on toe
we become a so and so.
Then the burden of house and mortgage
to survive we forage.

With sounds of tiny footsteps
to see we soon need specs.
Life soon takes its toll
with age from side to side we roll.

Childhood memories soon fade
under hovering dark shade.
We enter the end of our earthly life
and close our eyes ending our strife.

Albert Moses

BLINK OF AN EYE

The stones of time, have built this land
The sands of time, are in our hand.
After a million years BC
How insignificant is me.
Our time upon this earth is small
And we don't really count at all.
And like a candle in a storm
A velvet rose, a bloody thorn
No wealth, or beauty, or cruelty stays
One whole lifetime, could just be days.
How small we are, how hard we fall,
And no one noticed us at all.

Sally M McNab

TIME IS PRECIOUS

Time is precious so they say
Passing quickly day by day
Can we have it back? No way
Let's not waste our time away.

When we're young the time goes slow
There is much we need to know
Learning lessons as we grow
Not yet reaping what we sow.

Into teens then adulthood
Finding partner if we would
Starting family if we could
Sharing all things as we should.

Soon we're on that merry-go-round
Join the rat-race, break new ground
Nose to grindstone like bloodhound
Working guts out - extra pound.

Now approaching middle age
Power, possessions all the rage
Second car and house mortgage
Ever seeking higher wage.

End of working life draws nigh
Soon put feet up - heave a sigh
Won't be sorry - will not cry
Had enough of 'do or die'.

Now at last we can retire
Pipe and slippers by the fire
Baggy sweater - old attire
Living life like country squire.

All too soon we're getting old
Friends are dying - homes are sold
What's the point of wealth untold
Time and health worth more than gold.

Keith Johnson

THE HOLLOW

Warm pain drips like blood
from a sea-soaked brain.
The tide is out now.
Ransacked and flung high,
drying to bone, crying the tune
of a lone star, cold in the night's wind.
The mind turns again to shallower things,
safe, staring pebbles rocked nearshore,
asleep but not to dream,
rephaim that never leave sheol;
soft-suck and whisper, the broken landbones of a grave.
Deep, deep in the ocean where black waters weigh suffocatingly
(can that ever have been home?)
still nautiloids play - quick-catch and hide now,
in the echoes of our game.
Where's the way? Where's the path and the lamp
you promised?
Where were your footprints in the sea?
How could I hear you call through the roaring?
It still fills my ears.
The desert creeps into my skin while I am waiting,
a dry sea of sand, wind-whistling.
It's just the same as the sea,
always changing, moving, confusing, calling.
Calling? Is that really my name?
But I only play games.
Follow without any road? Only one hollow lying warm
away from the sea,
just near enough to reach but away from the sea.
That's no way, no way. No way.

Jane Upchurch

FOR MANDY (SWEET CHILD)

Sweet child, I see upon your face my own
That same enchantment in your eyes I knew
And while reflecting on my saddest thought
I take another searching look at you.
Your eyes are bright, yet in their depth I see
Reflections of the sad child sometimes me.
You turn and smile, and I remember well
The happiness of summer days long gone,
When every morn held wonder and surprise;
When every evening ended with a song.
Enjoy your childhood little girl of mine
For life gives sadness in its sweetest wine.

Rita E M Hunter

WHAT COMES AFTER?

Maybe one day I shall find out
Just what it's all about
Why are we here at all?
It makes me bang my head against the wall.

How did the elephant and the flea
Both starting as a dot in the sea
Grow so far apart in size?
It gives speculation to rise.

Why do some creatures have feathers
And others only skin that weathers?
Why are shrimps still in the sea?
It's all a puzzle to me.

Helen Cronin

MAINTENANCE

I was paying already, but they wanted more.
Screwed me for every penny, I worked hard for.
My life destroyed, and down on my luck,
I took the easiest way out, stood in the path of a truck.
It hit me full force, shedding its load,
Sending me careering and tumbling, down the busy main road.

When I awake, I'm on a bed.
I see lights flashing above my head.
A transparent covering around my face.
Tubes up my nose, tied with lace.

As nurses argue about their pay,
Precious seconds tick away.
The doctor's questions are like a quiz,
But by then I'd lost my will to live.
The pain was so great, I closed my eyes,
And begged the doctors, to let me die.

One of them, asks me my name,
But all I can do is scream with pain.
'Morphine nurse, 30 milligrams fast.
To save this man, that is my task.'
I see my life flash before me, then a light of brilliant white.
A long beep from the monitor, gives everyone a fright.

Suddenly, it all went dark.
I saw my children playing in the park.
I see them crying above a grave.
On the stone, Ron Peterson neatly engraved.

Indiana, Patrick, Aaron, Corrine and Shawn,
Poor little children, for now they mourn.
A loving, caring father, taken away.
Thanks to the unsympathetic nature of the CSA.

Ron R Peterson

DEPARTING

O she is dark and she is fair!
How dark her hair, how pale her face,
In her embrace there's no despair.

I glimpse her from my wood of care.
She waits beyond in moonlit grace.
O she is dark and she is fair!

From gloom I limp to meet her there.
How grave her air, how calm her gaze,
In her embrace there's no despair.

She takes my arm and on we fare
On silver grass through silver haze.
O she is dark and she is fair!

A river flows, the ripples flare,
All dark beyond. So this the place . . .
In her embrace there's no despair.

We mount the arch and I'm aware
That I must cross and she retrace.
O she is dark and she is fair!
In her embrace there's no despair.

John Hatton Davidson

FROM THE CRADLE TO THE GRAVE

The infant born into his mother's arms
Small and beautiful he can do no harm
To fend for himself, he isn't able
He can only cry and smile in his cradle
Listening and learning how to talk
He starts to crawl before he can walk

Then he reaches the stage of a boy
He then quickly grows out of his toys
He finds other interests and hobbies at school
But still he's wrapped up in mother's cotton wool
Like a young bird learning to fly
He's willing to give these new things a try

The teenage years are hardest; it's usually the case
When spots and hair start to sprout on his face
The time when girls come into the picture
How to handle it all, he's not too sure
He can start turning obnoxious and rude
This is the first taste of adulthood

On his mother, he's no longer dependant
He's a man now; he's independent
Getting married and starting a family
They're his pride and joy as he watches over them happily
He teaches them what he was told
Now he watches the process of their lives unfold

Growing old and reaching pension age
He's always dreaded this stage
He sees it happening all over again
As his grandchildren go through those growing pains
His wisdom, it's that a lot of people crave
A lifetime of experience from the cradle to the grave.

Twinny

MIDDLE DEATH

Hurtling along to meet it head on
Too late now for the end he had seen
Beautiful life cut off before time
Romantically passing away

Too soon it will be for the logical close
To a complete and quiet existence
In a white dream it waits darkly obscene
Middle aged,
Middle life,
Middle death.

Not quite dead in a hospital bed
Shapes move about
Moths to a light could put the flame out

Fighting for breath they deny him his death
With cellophane bags
And cake-icing needles plunged into his back

Painted green for the X-ray machine
That dulls his brain forgetting his name

Friends come to stare
They don't dare
To touch for fear of infection

Clutching their posies of tulips and roses
The pretty bunched smells don't smother the yells
As they bleed for their roots

They move away
Their good deed for the day
Weep for a while so again they can smile

When he is dead they clear the bed
In anticipation of the next in line
For weary consternation.

Elisabeth Ware

TIME AND TIDE

And now the passing has begun
2000 years before the sun,
learning times repeat their score
first there was peace and then there was war.
But nature was pure when reason took flight
and history fixed its constant light,
nations dared by their people brought fate
on centuries sure path part crooked part straight.
Invention stirred to excite the blind
and sinew stretched the inquisitive mind,
from art and crafts hewn the standard - raw
and each new face enlarged that swelling store.
Each saviour waved their guiding hand
whilst others carved a promised land,
and golden voices so charmed in few
their rituals served and the masses grew.
2000 summers have passed before
what stirs our existence unlocks a new door,
what happened can't change - the moment was laid
tasks and choices for the future to be made.
Ask not for more save knowledge should grow
if tolerance be fractured and spirit be slow,
draw to a lesson let wisdom ordain
conquer with pride and fight evil's pain.
Like a single yarn that curls thro' life
in fear of division by the cut of a knife,
look far ahead upon risks we must tether
a dominion unknown we enter together.
Uncharted dawn awaits mankind
a threshold before us in the dark to find,
who knows this millennium - a chapter to fill
where promises in flood bubble to a thrill.
Each age has endured those people it bore
they championed reform took wonder and more,

each born to their instincts shaped culture for their time
endeavoured to recall the fanciful and sublime.
Now left to unscramble a reflective eye
in an evening of thought finished in a sigh,
a brief recollection stored as milled grain
reserved for need when need comes again.
The mantle moves on let us wish it well
will our force survive who can know who can tell,
will our fragile notions belie infant cries
say that last blade of grass wilts and dies.

Tom Griffiths

SHE LIVES

Earth is our planet; a jewel . . .
       Of spinning beauty in the universe;
Our home, to be cherished
       By us, for her priceless worth.

Turbulent seas and mighty oceans wide,
       Rivers deep and trickling streams;
That contribute to all life on earth,
       Are, no longer what they have once been.

Only an unknowing observer,
       Looking down from far out in space,
Could fail to know, the quality of all life
       Upon our world, has seen much better days.

Species of life dying needlessly,
       Because of the things that we do;
Upsetting the balance of continuation,
       This beautiful planet . . . once knew.

For Earth, our true home, is as vibrantly alive
       As we, who walk upon her face;
As such, she should be cherished . . .
       In each heart, hold her rightful place.

When hearts love and embrace the earth,
       As a living needing creation;
She can continue to live, and support life;
       The true mother of every nation.

Maureen Annette Norman

OLD AGE

I overheard a chance remark,
Someone said 'He's too old.'
It isn't me, it couldn't be.
I'd know - or I'd be told!

I haven't got an aching back,
I don't ache anywhere
My teeth don't ache - they've all dropped out
And where the hell's my hair?

Yes, I can see, my eyes are good,
My hearing's not changed much.
What's that you say? TV's too loud?
Couldn't see which knob to touch!

I don't need help from anyone,
I'm capable and sane.
Oh - could you get my Zimmer frame -
I need the loo again.

Did you say *'Old'*? Watch your manners young man
I blame it on Old Father Time.
Not me, my dear lad, not me, I'm not old
I'm 90 and just in my prime.

Gwen Stone

INFANCY'S PINNACLE

There's a mountain in our bathroom,
They all call it the toilet.
I don't care what its name is,
I only want to climb it!
Stood on the floor
I reach, to the back
And the handhold there
Enables me, to scrabble
Up the slippery pan face where,
I can stretch, one knee upon the rim,
The other's dangling in the air!
A grab for the bath, grip it tight.
This, is, a struggle, but this time
I might, make it to the top . . .

Jacquie L Smith

MY HISTORY BEARS WITNESS

My history bears witness
To where my fears stem from
Naturally I am scared
Fearful of past events
That dominate my mind and my thought processes
I want
I need
Someone to bring peace
Peace to a heart that knows only hatred
I know hatred
Because that is what I am regularly faced with
Presently my soul is dirtied with past sins
Which can only be cleansed, cleaned with prayer.

Naeem Mirza

SEA GAZERS

On the beach as a child, sandy kneed full of glee,
there were deckchairs of old folk gazing straight out to sea.

So I stood, watched and waited always in vain,
to see what enthralled them, then returned to my game.

In my teens silly giggling, flirty eyed at the boys,
still they sat there engrossed, unaware of our noise.

As a mum with small children busy eyed on the sands,
I envied their peace and dried bodies and hands.

Now I am retired, children grown out of reach,
so I take myself off for a walk by the beach.

I look at the old folks gazing soft out to sea,
and realise with much wonder, that one of them's me.

Lesley Gill

THE LAST STAGE

Death . . .

Someone you love
Dying suddenly,
No warning,
Alive, warm,
Caring, loving;
Dead, cold,
Unable to care,
Unable to love;
Gone . . . just like that!

Death . . .

A slow, painful,
Living death,
Causing resentment,
Causing pain,
Ending
In quick, sudden,
Jerking death,
Gone . . . at last!

Death . . .

Death through old age,
Slowly losing
The grasp on life,
Slipping away,
Quietly, peacefully;
Gone . . . but expected.

Death.

Janet D Reeve

TRAPPED IN OLD AGE

Where do we go from here,
Now love has gone cold,
Our children have left us
Young love has turned old.

Our bodies are wrinkled,
Our hair has turned grey,
Our hearts have withered,
And we're counting each day.

Time has departed,
Our youth has fled,
We're not the same people
We were when we wed.

We're too old to finish,
Alive enough to see,
I don't love you,
You no longer love me.

We're two old people,
Trapped through our age,
Two great actors,
Performing on stage.

Claire Partridge

WHY?

Why do we love who we do?
Please give me the answers -
I'm asking
Why do I love, yes, you?

Why do we act as we do?
We quarrel and argue -
I'm asking
Because I still haven't a clue!

Why do we regret what we've done?
The web we have spun
Can't be undone
And yet through it all, I love you!

I asked you when I was small,
But I haven't the answers at all.
We still go on,
Knowing right, doing wrong -
And yet I still say, I love you!

Oh, God, can you forgive,
Our pride and our greed
As we live;
The mistakes we have made;
And we have paid!
And with it all, you still say -
'I love you!'

Beatrice Wilson

CHRYSALIS

In the darkest room you're growing
an embryo, encased, cocooned,
chrysalis waiting to emerge
new life within the womb.

Nine months gently cradled there
in warmth and solitude,
it's time, the membrane breaks,
pushing life into the room.

Naked in his parents' arms,
awakens breath towards the dawn
engulfed in life's eternal love,
their baby boy is born.

Eily Tatlow

SIMPLE LIFE 1998

I feel happiness everywhere,
I love to watch the rain,
I love to watch the snow flying,
I love to watch the leaves falling in the autumn,
I love to watch the sea crashing against the rocks,
I love to watch the cars passing by my window,
I love to watch the stars blushing in the night sky,
I love to watch people smiling as they pass.
I love my life,
Such a simple life.

Donna Joanne Kinsey

BEGINNINGS

it was yet dark
aeons ago:
embryo eternities
seeds wait
to breathe/grow

    time awakens slowly
    empty world
    wind trembles
    not yet unfurled
    living seeds wait

in darkness curled
quite alone
seeking to give life
to stone:
footprints appear

    he took clay
    moulded it soft
    fingerprints allow
    time to live

footprints go forward
sad wind stops
he cries into eternity
soul is set free

    sun hangs a lantern
    lights darkness
    footsteps are shaped
    life has begun

uncurling like fossils
learning about life
they dream near fire
watching future in stars

T Webster

AS A YOUNG BOY

I worked in the forest most of my young life
I was making charcoal I did this job until I was 18.
I started at 9 years old.
Then I thought that I had had enough of hard work
and solitude. I wanted to change so I left the forest.
Since then I have been happy and content, but
I must confess I do miss the forest,
mostly the life outside and the open fire.
In my little wooden hut the winter months were too long.
Sometimes I told myself that I was the only human
in the world because I never saw anyone until the
snow last.
Outside was cold and nasty but in the hut it was so
warm and cosy.
The shortage of food was most difficult.
When the snow started to fall I would not see anyone.
Only the wild animals kept me company day and night,
but in the summertime the forest was like a paradise.

Antonio Martorelli

AUTUMNAL

Across the sleeping meadowland
I see your eyes in pools of dew
And recall the summer days with you,
The darkness of your hair all around
And a star falling.

Within the winding woodland ways,
Your voice a caress in the wind's low moan
In the branches whispers 'Summer is gone.'
The trees are weeping for bygone days
And the leaves falling.

Beyond the woods, the kindling sun
Brushes the gloom from a brooding hill,
I remember your warmth, and I feel a chill
For a shadow is on me, yet night is done
And the light falling.

J C Fearnley

GIFTED

On father's arm
gifted in pleasure,
to take another's name
his precious treasure,
lighting the inward eye
kindled in heady days,
cradled, protected
under paternal rays,
dandled on childish rhymes,
shouldered on high,
held tight through nightmares
swung to the sky,
taught how to skate
and ski in the snow,
there in the background
minding her go,
proud in achievement
pleased for her gain,
wanting pure happiness
wishing no pain.
Now to release her
as woman and wife,
to live with her chosen
the love of her life.

Shirley Johnson

UNTITLED

She looked out beyond what was
Maybe she was thinking
About what had become of it all
Or maybe she was scared
For what was about to be

She looked in the child's eyes
Maybe trying to retrace
But nothing came of it
And the space beyond became
The place to think once again

Maybe she will get to wherever
She was going having discovered
What she was searching for
But her look said
'Still waiting'

Shaun Geary

IN OUR MINDS

In our minds and in our hearts
the memories and feelings of the years past,
those memories and stories oh what they meant to me,
those unforgotten times again will never be.
Together in this world, young and old
we saw the brave conquered by the bold
but understandingly times were hard
well it was unavoidable with a world so large.
Now at a certain point I felt like breaking down,
for in this world's great struggle, it was hard to get around
the things we did and didn't do,
oh yes both together me and you.
The things we did and didn't see,
the days of being captured and the days of being free.

Now in my mind I can see it,
I can hear it when I'm in an empty room,
in my dreams I can feel it,
yes see the people, all the ones I ever knew.
Now I wonder what each new day brings,
around every corner a wonder of new things,
now all my youth has gone away, all I have left
are those memories of yesterday . . .

D G Morgan

THE PAST *OR* WHERE I WOULD BE

Summers were always long and hot in childhood days,
nights in close quarters with siblings,
breathless with the heat, as tiny windows hung with ramblers,
stopped the buzzing air, sheets then were tied to bed posts,
knobs of brass or wood made tents exciting,
heard of only in the magic of an Arabian tale.

Paddling in streams and rivers as yet unspoiled by polluted
foam only the green of sharp leafed watercress as the
waters babbled by. Dragonflies hovering,
darting over stagnant pools,
small lizards easing out from under sandy stones.
Days to lay back on stubbled straw watching the birds
soar timelessly above thick meadow grass.

But winter's biting cold, as frosts and snow combined;
stomping to school in rubber wellingtons, with chilblains . . .
through passages forged through solid snow,
arriving just in time for milk thawed against pot-bellied
stove with lumps of ice still in the freezing bottles.
For sport, snow thrown in balls, or slip-slides made on paths.
A peril to our elders.
When canals froze over, they became our skating rinks
where in balmier days horse-drawn barges had ambled by.
These were the days when winter sport cost nothing
but an old wood tray, when injury was repaired by the
stinging dab of iodine.

And summer's cost was an elasticated suit of red or blue,
or hand-kit wool that stretched and pulled when weighted
down with water from the stream.

But spring and autumn had their rightful place.
Seasons were seasons in our youth.
In spring the hedgerows for the boys, 'Birds nesting',
our clout could not be cast even on the mildest day
until the month had passed, of May,
even though we fast approached the longest day.

Autumn the time of harvest festivals, Thanksgivings,
collecting wood for bonfires.
Home was the place of cooking smells and pots of jam
where Mother reigned supreme, her offerings fondly
garnished with acts of love.
Home was complete when Father bent his head to enter
after a hard day of toil, and said the grace and carved the meat,
then told wild tales of his exciting youth.

This is the place where I would be, memories do not need
storage space, shelf room, only a quiet corner and a comfy chair.
All of my friends can afford to be with me, no great expense
to travel: just the desire and the will to be there . . .

The Painter In Words

INFORMATION

We hope you have enjoyed reading this book - and that you will continue to enjoy it in the coming years.

If you like reading and writing poetry drop us a line, or give us a call, and we'll send you a free information pack.

Write to :-
Poetry Now Information
1-2 Wainman Road
Woodston
Peterborough
PE2 7BU
(01733) 230746